LITTLE MY'S
book of thoughts

ILLUSTRATIONS AND QUOTATIONS BY TOVE JANSSON
TEXT BY SAMI MALILA
TRANSLATION BY OLIVER WASTIE

Excerpts and illustrations by Tove Jansson © Moomin Characters Ltd., Finland
Text © Sami Malila and WSOY
Original title: "Pikku Myyn mietekirja"
First published in Finnish by Werner Söderström Corporation (WSOY) in 2005,
Helsinki, Finland
Translation into English © Oliver Wastie
First published in English by SelfMadeHero in 2011
A division of Metro Media Ltd
5 Upper Wimpole Street London W1G 6BP
www.selfmadehero.com

Publishing Director: Emma Hayley
Marketing Director: Doug Wallace
Editorial Assistant: Lizzie Kaye
Cover Designer: Kurt Young
With thanks to: Nick de Somogyi

This work has been published with the financial assistance of
FILI – Finnish Literature Exchange

A CIP record for this book is available from the British Library

978-1-906838-20-1

10 9 8 7 6 5 4 3 2 1

Printed and bound in China

To the Reader

The beloved Moomin stories of Tove Jansson are full of thrilling adventures, exuberant humour, eternal truths and timeless wisdom.

This is a collection of Little My's thoughts and surprising insights into the world around her. Little My can be so direct that she sometimes needs to be kept in line. Little My also knows how to ask difficult questions and give confident answers. She has a unique talent for encouraging others to be independent and brave.

We hope you enjoy the wise words and enchanting insights of Little My's Book of Thoughts!

Excerpts and illustrations are from the following WSOY editions of the Moomin books, translated from the original Swedish into Finnish:

VAARALLINEN JUHANNUS

TAIKATALVI

NÄKYMÄTÖN LAPSI JA MUITA KERTOMUKSIA

MUUMIPAPAN UROTYÖT

MUUMIPAPPA JA MERI

KUINKAS SITTEN KÄVIKÄÄN? KIRJA MYMMELISTÄ,
MUUMIPEIKOSTA JA PIKKU MYYSTÄ

Contents

Little My's
Insights and Observations

LITTLE My jumped from her sister's shoulder onto a shelf. She peered into the mirror and shouted: "Hey, look! I've become even smaller. I can't see myself at all any more!"

"BUT I want to swell up and become large – I want to, want to, want to!" shouted Little My.

Slowly, an angry face with dishevelled hair peeked out from the hole in the cover of the cardboard box.

"Is your head made of stuffing?" said Little My.

"No, I don't think so," replied the squirrel.

"Now you've woken me up," continued Little My vehemently. "What's more, you've eaten my sleeping bag. What exactly do you think you are playing at?"

Then Little My went out of the cave to examine the winter. The first thing she did was to slip on the icy hill and fall over backwards with a thud.

"I see," said Little My in a menacing voice. "So it's like that, is it?" Then it crossed her mind as to what a My would look like with a pair of feet pointing up towards the sky, and she laughed to herself for a long time. She looked at the hill and pondered. Then she said, "Let's see!" and sitting on her bottom she sped all the way down the steep hill, over bumps and everything, without stopping until she was way out on the glimmering ice.

"WHEN you're angry, then you're angry," thought Little My, peeling her potato with her teeth. "Sometimes you have to be angry. Every little creature has the right to get angry."

"MOTHERS don't just disappear like that for no reason," said Little My. "They're always in some corner – if you just look."

"I'M not going to say a word about mothers and fathers," said Little My with deliberate slowness. "Because you will immediately say that mothers and fathers can never be silly. Now they're playing some game or other, but I'll be damned if I understand what it is."

"But you don't need to understand," said Moomintroll angrily. "They know themselves why they are being strange. Some people always have to try and gain the upper hand just because they happen to be adopted."

"You've hit the nail on the head," said Little My. "I always *do* have the upper hand."

"WELL, well, well," said Little My with interest. "Moominpappa is angry. He's letting it all out!"

"NOW you look as though you've come to the wrong party," said Little My.

"WHAT are you waiting for? Praise, or what?" shouted Little My. "Don't you have any spark about you, or what? Do you want me to give you a really good thrashing?"

"Please don't," squeaked Ninny humbly.

"She doesn't know how to play," said Moomintroll in embarrassment.

"She doesn't know how to get angry," said Little My. "That's what is wrong with her. Listen," continued My, and went right up to Ninny and looked at her threateningly. "You'll never get your own face unless you learn to fight. Believe me."

"BELIEVE me, I'm terribly wise!" said Little My.

"YOU shouldn't pity everyone so much," said Little My. "Now leave me alone. I'm going to curl up for a while."

LITTLE My shrugged her shoulders and crawled back into the moss. She had often seen people standing and waiting for each other in the wrong place, stupidly and hopelessly. It can't be helped; perhaps it is just meant to be.

"Don't you think he was a little strange?" asked Moominpappa hesitantly.

"He was very strange," insisted Little My. "Totally bonkers."

Moominmamma sighed and tried to straighten out her legs. "But so are most of our friends," she said, "to some degree or other."

"You're so conventional!" complained Little My. She stood by the window and looked out dejectedly. "And I thought things were going to be different here..."

LITTLE My took in a gulp of air through her nose and pushed it out between her teeth.

"That fisherman is barmy, he has seaweed for brains," she said. "I realized that instantly. And if two barmy people live on the same island, then they either know everything about each other or else they don't want to know anything about each other at all. Or most likely the former and the latter. In other words: they don't want to know, because they know already."

LITTLE My turned around at the door and said:
"I intend to sleep outside – without a bed. Beds are silly."

On Dangers and Mishaps

"I THINK WE'RE IN TROUBLE NOW," SAID LITTLE MY.

"Everything will burn to a crisp!" shouted Little My happily. "And everybody's houses and gardens and toys and little sisters and playthings will burn!"

"Nonsense," said Moominmamma in a friendly tone as she brushed the soot off her nose.

"Diabolical pandemonium will break out here – you mark my words."

"I'M not even afraid of ants!" replied Little My, and she sat up.

"OF course they'll find their way home! They're sure to find their way home!" said Moominmamma.

"Unless someone has eaten them," said Little My. "I'm sure the ants will have bitten them so that now they are larger than oranges!"

"BUT, my friends," said Little My, "ants are like mosquitoes, and it's best just to squash them."

MOOMINPAPPA set off down the mountainside. Little My was jumping around him like a flea; she shouted something that was taken by the wind as it rushed past.

"THAT fir tree is sheltering the little birch tree in order to save it," said Moomintroll.

"That's what you think," said Little My darkly. "I think it's not going to let it out of its clutches. This is just the type of forest from which nothing escapes. I wouldn't be at all surprised if there was someone deep in the forest in a bit of a squeeze – like this!" She grabbed Moomintroll's neck with her arms, and squeezed.

"YOU blow your top at just about everything, don't you?" said Little My with contempt.

Wonders and Enigmas

"Is this the end of the world?" asked Little My inquisitively.

"At the very least," said the Mymble's daughter, "try and be good if it's possible, because we will soon all be going to heaven."

"Heaven?" repeated Little My. "Do we *have* to go to heaven? And how will we get back from there?"

"I see, so this is what it looks like," said Little My. "Whatever next?!" She immediately made a snowball and threw it with some accuracy at the squirrel.

"HEY, something is crawling into my lap," said Little My in surprise, looking at her empty lap.

THE invisible shrews rushed out, bringing some hot water, and wrapped the squirrel in a warm towel. But his stiff little paws stood just as rigidly and forlornly in the air, and not a single tuft of fur moved.

"He's well and truly dead," said Little My matter-of-factly.

"At least he got to see something really beautiful before he died," whispered Moomintroll in a quivering voice.

"Well," said Little My. "Be that as it may, he has in any case forgotten everything now. And I intend to make a lovely little muff from his tail."

"Now it's going out," said Little My. "Put some more paper on it." She was sitting on the railings, shaded by the veranda pillar.

"So that's where you've been hiding," said Moominpappa, and he shook the ashtray until the flame went out. "I'm examining the science of fire – it's important."

My laughed and looked at him intently. Then Pappa pulled his hat over his eyes and escaped into sleep.

LITTLE My took a deep breath in through her nose and let it out between her teeth in a very unpleasant manner, which meant to say, "I've never heard anything so stupid in all my life."

"SOME people are in such a good mood," said Little My. "It would be better if some people kept an eye on their whisky crate."

"OF course, everything is wonderful," said Little My. "More or less. The most amazing thing would be if we were to make a big song and dance about moving there with all our belongings only to discover that the whole island was in fact only a speck of dirt on the map."

How to Make Life
Fun and Exciting

"LITTLE My has been picking milk cap mushrooms again," said Moominpappa. "Last year she picked death caps."

"Let's hope that she picks chanterelles next year," said Moominmamma. "Or at least some field mushrooms."

"It's good to live in hope," said Little My, sniggering to herself.

LITTLE My was sitting on the steps and singing her monotonous rain song – or one of them.

"Hello," said Moominpappa. "I'm angry!"

"That's good," said Little My approvingly. "You appear to have gained a suitable enemy; it might make you feel better."

"I also have a secret," said Snufkin. "It's in my rucksack. You can see what it is in a while. Because then I'm going to settle an old score with a crook!"

"A big or a small one?" asked Little My.

"A small one," replied Snufkin.

"That's good," said Little My. "It's more fun to deal with small crooks that break easily."

LITTLE My was jumping up and down on the other side, like a ball, and they understood that she was shouting "hurrah" to them.

"CAN I cut up your ball of wool?" shouted Little My from the sewing basket.

"HERE we go," said Little My, spreading her skirt into the malicious north wind. She started to glide here and there in between the patches of snow, braced her legs and kept her balance with assurance, as Mys usually do.

THE snow crunched under their paws, and their breath rose like white smoke from their mouth. Moomintroll's snout became so stiff that he couldn't wrinkle it.

"This isn't for the faint-hearted," said Little My with delight, as she skipped across the frozen shore.

"PUT me on your head so that I can jump off if we don't make it."

She grabbed a firm hold of Moomintroll's ears and shouted: "Company, towards the shore, about-turn!"

Respecting Differences

"I never realized you had eyebrows," said Little My curiously. "Now they have turned white, and you look even more surprised than ever."

"If I am sad, I don't need to show it with a mourning band," said Little My.

"That's right if you are sad – but you aren't sad," said Moomintroll.

"No I'm not," said Little My. "I don't know how to be. I'm only ever happy or angry. Would it help the squirrel if I were sad?"

BECAUSE Moominmamma had noticed on going up to the wall that she had been painted no bigger than a coffee pot, she added several small Moominmammas here and there in the garden to make sure that she could be seen in the landscape. If she could only remain quiet, the others would hardly be able to tell which Moominmamma was the right one.

"Well now, there's an unhealthy need for recognition," said Little My looking at the wall. "Couldn't you paint us as well and not just yourself?"

MOOMINPAPPA came down the ladder and said, "The wind has turned slightly north-northeast. Maybe it will start to die down. I've been thinking that we should really invite that fisherman round for coffee one of these days."

"I bet he doesn't drink coffee," said Little My. "I think he only eats seaweed and raw fish. Perhaps he filters plankton through his front teeth."

"What are you talking about?" exclaimed Moominmamma. "What strange tastes!"

"Precisely – seaweed," repeated Little My. "That's how he seems, anyway. I wouldn't be at all surprised. But he is independent and never asks anything," she added respectfully.

"And he doesn't tell you anything either?" asked Moominpappa.

"Not the slightest thing," said Little My.

On Fear and Fearlessness

"HE'S A CROOK!" WHISPERED LITTLE MY. "HE'S ONLY
WAITING SO THAT HE CAN BUMP US OFF!"

"TELL them if they don't behave, you'll set the Groke on them!" suggested Little My. "That's what my sister does."

"Does it work on you?"

"Of course not!" said Little My, and she laughed so hard that she fell over.

"THE Groke," continued Little My pensively. "That large, cold Groke wanders around, sitting down here and there... And do you know what happens to the spot where she has been sitting?"

"I bet the Groke has eaten him!" shouted Little My. "Or else he's fallen down a hole and been squashed!"

"THEY'RE afraid," said Little My, looking directly at Moomintroll. "They are so afraid that every single pine needle is standing on end; they're even more afraid than you!"

"DID you think I was scowling at you?" asked Little My innocently. "Why? Perhaps I was scowling at something behind you..."

Moomintroll jumped with fright and turned around.

"Ha-hah! I was only kidding!" shrieked Little My with glee. "What are you so frightened of?"

"SHUSH! I can hear something," said Little My from the front of the boat. "Keep quiet for a moment, there's something going on."

LITTLE My was hanging dangerously out of the north-facing window without a care in the world.

LITTLE My was jumping up and down for joy, her bun had come open in the storm, and her hair was flying about her like a spiky halo.

EVERY now and then a rumble could be heard, like a cannon shot fired in celebration and destruction, sending cold shivers of exhilaration up and down Little My's back.

"I hope those bores don't come and rescue me," she thought. "It would spoil everything."

SNUFKIN pointed with his pipe. A small saucepan of peas was bubbling away on the camp fire, and next to it was some hot coffee in another pot. "But I guess you only drink milk?" he said.

Little My laughed with contempt. As quick as a flash, she poured herself two full teaspoons of coffee and ate four whole peas.

The Amazing Little My

IT'S STRANGE HOW DEFTLY MYS ALWAYS MANAGE TO GET
THEMSELVES OUT OF A TIGHT SPOT.

MIDSUMMER Night came and went (incidentally, the Mymble's smallest daughter was born on that very same day and given the name My, which means "the smallest thing possible").

LITTLE My's plate was of course very small, and it was in the middle of the table shaded by a vase.

"IS the coffee ready?" asked Little My. "I always get really thirsty in a storm."

LITTLE My was as usual on her own somewhere, but nobody really needed to worry about her. She probably dealt with the situation better than anyone else in the family.

"LITTLE My is used to looking after herself," said the Mymble's daughter. "I would be more worried about anyone who finds themselves in her firing line!"

LITTLE My sat laughing somewhere in one of her numerous hiding places, and her sister knew it.

"She should lure me with some honey," thought Little My. "And then give me a walloping when I come out."

"She always does exactly what she wants and nobody goes against her. That's just how she is."

LITTLE My had always been able to have fun on her own, and it seemed that she didn't feel the need to tell the others how she felt about the spring.

"PAH! Do you think that I'm some old gossip?" said Little My. "I'm not so interested in other people's secrets that I could be bothered to go around spreading them. In any case, sooner or later people always give them away themselves."

"HEY, older sister," shouted Little My, slapping the Mymble on the back. But she just kept on sleeping and didn't move a muscle. "Now I'm getting cross," said Little My. "The one time when I would have needed a sister!"

ONCE the fire in the stove was alight, Little My slipped in through a crack in the door and jumped onto the windowsill like a cat. She pressed her nose against the glass and made ugly faces at the swallows.

IT is possible Little My had observed Moomintroll and had all kinds of opinions on the matter, but nobody would have known.

LITTLE My jumped up like lightning, but Moominpappa grabbed her by her bun. "I don't think so," he said. "This time you're not going first."

"Oh, I see," said Little My. "Well that's just what I thought."

And that was the end of the matter. Little My banged a large nail all the way into the wood and whistled through the gap in her teeth.

"It's amazing that they can be so fierce," said Little My in admiration.

"I'll arrange it," said Little My calmly. "You can go there and take a look in a few days' time."

Little My nodded so furiously her bun wobbled.

The End